Visual Geography Series®

MADAGASCAR

...in Pictures

Prepared by
Geography Department

Lerner Publications Company
Minneapolis

Independent Picture Service

A wrestling match attracts a large crowd in Madagascar.

This is an all-new edition of the Visual Geography
Series. Previous editions have been published by Ster-
ling Publishing Company, New York City, and some
of the original textual information has been retained.
New photographs, maps, charts, captions, and updated
information have been added. The text has been en-
tirely reset in 10/12 Century Textbook.

LIBRARY OF CONGRESS CATALOGING-IN-PUBLICATION DATA

Madagascar in pictures / prepared by Geography
  Department, Lerner Publications Company.
    p. cm. — (Visual geography series)
    Rev. ed. of: Madagascar / by Bernadine Bailey, and
others.
    Includes index.
    Summary: Introduces the land, history, government,
people, and economy of the republic occupying the
fourth largest island in the world.
    ISBN 0-8225-1841-4 (lib. bdg.)
    1. Madagascar. [1. Madagascar.] I. Bailey, Berna-
dine, 1901- . Madagascar. II. Lerner Publications
Company. Geography Dept. III. Series: Visual
geography series (Minneapolis, Minn.)
DT469.M26A585 1988   87-26629
969'.1—dc19   CIP
                                              AC

International Standard Book Number: 0-8225-1841-4
Library of Congress Catalog Card Number: 87-26629

VISUAL GEOGRAPHY SERIES®

Publisher
Harry Jonas Lerner
Associate Publisher
Nancy M. Campbell
Senior Editor
Mary M. Rodgers
Editor
Gretchen Bratvold
Assistant Editors
Dan Filbin
Kathleen S. Heidel
Illustrations Editor
Karen A. Sirvaitis
Consultants/Contributors
Philip Allen
Sandra K. Davis
Designer
Jim Simondet
Cartographer
Carol F. Barrett
Indexer
Kristine S. Schubert
Production Manager
Gary J. Hansen

Independent Picture Service

**Women in Antsirabe, a city in central Madagascar, sell
their produce at a weekly market.**

Acknowledgments

Title page photo by Alton Halverson.

Elevation contours adapted from *The Times Atlas of
the World,* seventh comprehensive edition (New York:
Times Books, 1985).

2   3   4   5   6   7   8   9   10   97   96   95   94   93   92   91   90   89

Farmers water their cattle—mostly zebu cows—at a river in Amboasary, southern Madagascar.

Contents

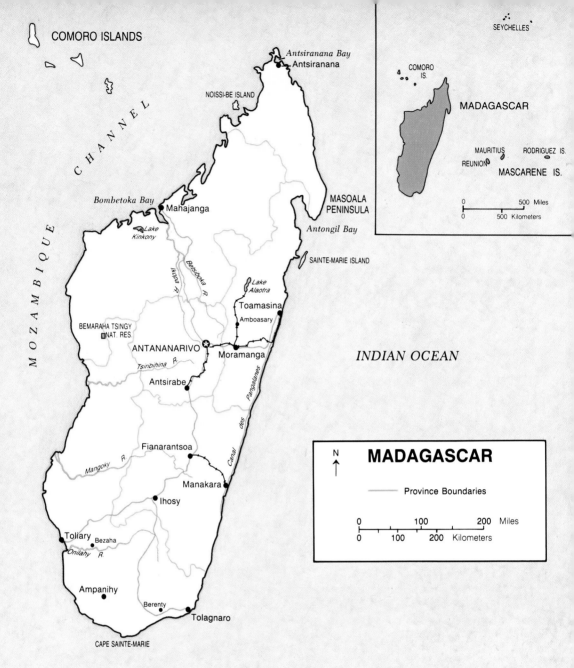

COMORO ISLANDS

Antsiranana Bay
Antsiranana

SEYCHELLES

COMORO
IS.

MADAGASCAR

MAURITIUS   RODRIGUEZ IS.
REUNION

MASCARENE IS.

0   500 Miles
0   500 Kilometers

NOISSI-BE ISLAND

C H A N N E L

M O Z A M B I Q U E

Bombetoka Bay
Mahajanga

*Lake
Kinkony*

Betsiboka R.

Ikopa R.

MASOALA
PENINSULA

Antongil Bay

SAINTE-MARIE ISLAND

*Lake
Alaotra*

Toamasina

Amboasary

BEMARAHA TSINGY
NAT. RES.

ANTANANARIVO

Moramanga

Tsiribihina R.

Antsirabe

Pangalanes

Canal des

INDIAN OCEAN

Fianarantsoa

Mangoky R.

Manakara

Ihosy

N

MADAGASCAR

—— Province Boundaries

0   100   200   Miles
0   100   200   Kilometers

Toliary
Bezaha
Onilahy R.

Ampanihy

Berenty

Tolagnaro

CAPE SAINTE-MARIE

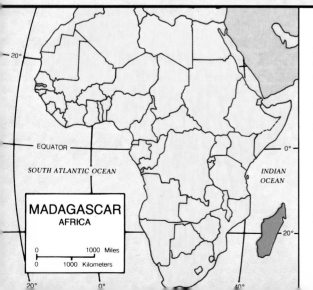

-20°

EQUATOR   0°

SOUTH ATLANTIC OCEAN

INDIAN
OCEAN

MADAGASCAR
AFRICA

0   1000 Miles
0   1000 Kilometers

20°   0°   40°

-20°

Gentle waves lap against a white-sand beach in Tolagnaro, a Malagasy city that faces the Indian Ocean.

Introduction

Madagascar, the large island that lies near Africa in the Indian Ocean, probably broke free from the continent more than 100 million years ago. For thousands of years, the land mass lay undisturbed as it inched away from the mainland of Africa.

When humans began to develop trade patterns many centuries ago, the island successively became known to Arab traders, Asian immigrants, and European explorers. Indeed, present-day Malagasy (the people of Madagascar) partly descend from Asians who migrated from what are now Indonesia and Malaysia more than 1,500 years ago. On their way to Madagascar, these travelers spent long periods of time in southern Asia, in East Africa, and probably on the nearby Comoro Islands.

Intermarriage between Asian and African peoples, as well as later immigrations of these ethnic groups, has created a varied population on the island. More recently, European colonial powers—particularly France—have introduced their cultures to the island. One legacy of French colonialism is the use of French as a second language. Malagasy is the national language.

Free of its colonial relationship with France since 1960, Madagascar further reduced its economic and political ties to France in 1972. In that year, military leaders overthrew the first independent government, and in 1975 the new government changed the official name of the country to the Democratic Republic of Madagascar. As a result of the coup d'état, Admiral Didier Ratsiraka became president—a post he continued to hold in 1989. Ratsiraka initiated socialist reforms—including widespread nationalization (government ownership) of private businesses—as well as far-reaching changes in foreign policy.

The Ratsiraka regime, however, has encountered many difficulties in putting its plans into action. The country has a massive foreign debt, which it is attempting to pay by increasing its output of goods for export. Political factions have held fast to their views, and the one-party system that the president hoped to achieve has not come to pass. Furthermore, his position has often been openly challenged.

More important perhaps is that Malagasy society itself remains seriously divided. Coastal inhabitants (collectively called *côtiers*) and people of the Central Highlands (called the Merina) distrust one another. Young Malagasy seem increasingly impatient with the inability of their elders to create opportunities for them. A wide gap exists between the few rich and the many poor. Prosperous businesspeople, landowners, and high-ranking government officials form a powerful class of Merina and côtier elites. These various groups resist Ratsiraka's ideas about redistributing the wealth of Madagascar.

Thus, Madagascar is a country that faces difficult problems. But it is also a nation with a rich culture, beautiful landscapes, and great economic possibilities. A fragile treasure-house of rare animals and plants, Madagascar is a land of contrasts. If its various subcultures can be persuaded to cooperate and if the energies of its people can be harnessed, then Madagascar may yet realize its vast potential.

Courtesy of American Lutheran Church

Cassavas—here being pounded into flour—have become a substitute staple food in Madagascar, which cannot grow enough rice to feed its population.

Buyers and sellers flock to the crowded market in Antananarivo, Madagascar's capital.

Much of Madagascar is underdeveloped, and people must continue to travel on foot along dirt roads.

Photo by Alton Halverson

A valley in Madagascar's central strip of highlands reveals the island's lush vegetation and agricultural possibilities.

1) The Land

Madagascar lies in the western Indian Ocean, 250 miles off the coast of Africa. The island once was connected to Africa, but it has developed in unique isolation since it separated from the continent more than 100 million years ago.

Madagascar is 1,000 miles long from north to south and has an average width of 250 miles. Its area of over 228,000 square miles—slightly smaller than the state of Texas—makes it the fourth largest island in the world. Only Greenland, New Guinea, and Borneo are larger.

Some of the island's nearest neighbors are other islands, including the Mascarene Islands (made up of Réunion, Mauritius, and Rodriguez) to the east, the Seychelles to the northeast, and the Comoro Islands to the north. Scientists believe that thousands of years ago the Comoros may have served as a land bridge between the African continent and Madagascar. The Mozambique Channel separates Madagascar from Africa and is about 240 miles wide at its narrowest point.

Topography

Madagascar's landscape is divided into three general regions: the east coast, the highlands, and the west coast. Each area is significantly different from the others in landscape features, access to the sea, and rainfall.

THE EAST COAST

Washed by waves from the Indian Ocean, the east coast of Madagascar is nearly straight, except for Antongil Bay and the Masoala Peninsula in the north. As a result, this shore has few natural harbors, and cyclones and coral reefs create hazardous shipping conditions. Indeed, the port of Toamasina is largely man-made. A 31-mile-wide band of lowlands leads to a section of steep cliffs and narrow valleys that eventually meets the highlands.

A feature of the east coast is the Canal des Pangalanes. Formed by currents of the Indian Ocean, the canal is a nearly 500-mile-long natural lagoon that hugs the coast and that has been used as a transportation sea-lane. The sandy beaches along the east coast slope quickly into shark-filled waters—a characteristic that has discouraged swimming and sailing.

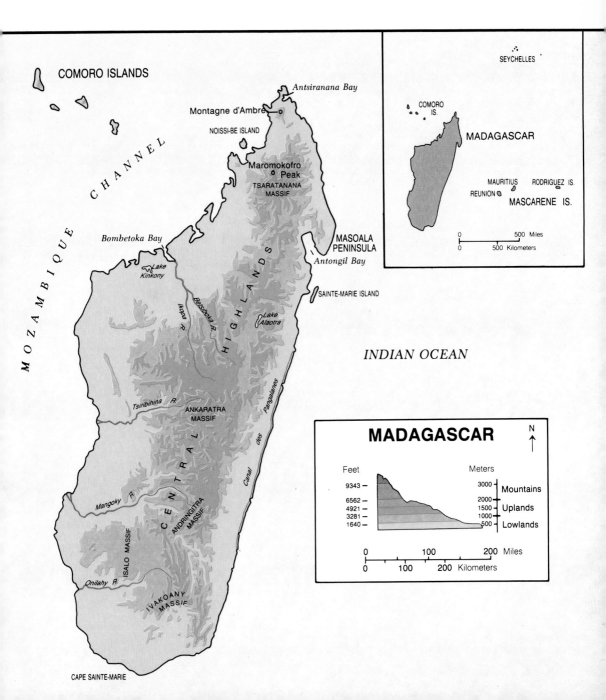

Courtesy of American Lutheran Church

Small, palm-ringed bays characterize Madagascar's western coast, which lies across the Mozambique Channel from the continent of Africa.

THE HIGHLANDS

Madagascar's mountainous areas, though largely confined to a long, middle strip of land (collectively called the Central Highlands), are clustered at the northern, central, and southern points of the island. Between the clusters are lower elevations with fertile valleys.

The Tsaratanana Massif (range) lies in the north and rises to heights of over 9,400 feet. This range contains the island's highest point—Maromokofro Peak, at 9,436 feet. North of the range, near the tip of the island, is Montagne d'Ambre, which is of volcanic origin. Sloping down from this massif is a deeply carved coastal region where the city of Antsiranana provides good port facilities. The mountains, however, prevent goods from reaching or leaving this part of the island by land.

Other mountain ranges appear hundreds of miles south of the Tsaratanana Massif. Near the very center of the island is the Ankaratra Massif, which contains the capital city of Antananarivo at 4,800 feet above sea level. To the southwest and southeast are the Isalo and Andringitra massifs, respectively. Near the southernmost tip lies the Ivakoany Massif. Located between the various mountain ranges are well-watered valleys or irrigated fields that produce most of the food grown on the island.

THE WEST COAST

The west coast—which lies across the Mozambique Channel from Africa—is far more indented and irregularly shaped than the east coast. The northern section features many small inlets and bays that are generally sheltered from harsh weather, such as cyclones. Because it holds a variety of possible sites for anchoring ships and because of its nearness to Africa, the west coast has attracted explorers and traders for many centuries. The soil on this coast is sedimentary (formed of rock fragments) and, in some places, has great agricultural potential.

Rivers and Lakes

Many rivers exist in Madagascar, but only a few make up the island's 1,550 miles of navigable waterways. The watershed—an elevated area that determines in which direction the rivers flow to reach their sea outlets—is less than 100 miles from the east coast. Consequently, the principal rivers flow to the west. The waterways traveling down the steep, eastern coast pass through deep gorges and ravines, creating numerous waterfalls.

The largest river in Madagascar, the Betsiboka, is navigable from the west coast for nearly 100 miles by lightweight steamers during the rainy season. Other major rivers are the Ikopa, the Mangoky, the Tsiribihina, and the Onilahy. The longest stretch of navigable water in Madagascar is the Canal des Pangalanes. Although 50-ton barges can use the canal, it has fallen into general disuse in recent years.

Along with saltwater lagoons, Madagascar has many freshwater lakes. Few, however, are large. The biggest are 25-mile-wide Lake Alaotra and Lake Kinkony, which is 16 miles wide. The remaining lakes are less than 10 miles wide. Scattered throughout the island are several crater-lakes, formed by the open cones of extinct volcanoes.

Climate

Located south of the equator, Madagascar lies in the tropics and receives shifting winds from the southeast. Its location gives the island two seasons—a hot, rainy season from November through March, and a cool, dry season from April through October.

Huge ocean deeps, ranging from 13,000 to 16,500 feet, lie directly off the east coast. Temperatures on this coast, where 30 percent of the Malagasy live, hover around 65° F and are ideal for growing important crops such as coffee, bananas, and vanilla. The climate is humid throughout the year, and over 110 inches of rain fall annually in the region. Severe cyclones strike the east coast between January and March, along with frequent floods.

The west coast is drier and receives less rainfall and fewer breezes. Rain occurs irregularly in the southern regions of the island and often measures as little as two inches annually in extreme southwestern areas of Madagascar.

Flora and Fauna

Madagascar's vegetation and animal life evolved separately from those of the nearby continent. As a result, the island's flora and fauna tell a unique evolutionary story. Many of the species on the island exist nowhere else in the world.

Unfortunately, the needs of the Malagasy to feed and house themselves have endangered this living laboratory. For example, farmers cut down and burn trees to make more room for pastureland and rice fields. Moreover, few efforts are made to replace the forests, which contain the island's unusual vegetation and animal habitats.

Less than 15,000 square miles of true forest remain in the island's 35,000 square miles of woodland. Nevertheless, it is estimated that 1,000 varieties of trees can still be found throughout Madagascar. Only in protected areas, such as Bemaraha Tsingy National Reserve, can the island's unique plants and wildlife remain safe from the advance of human settlement.

Waterfalls are a common feature along many of the island's rivers, which generally flow to the west.

Blooming jacaranda trees form a canopy of color on a main thoroughfare in Antananarivo.

Photo by Alton Halverson

FLORA

In certain hot areas, the raffia and other varieties of palms flourish. The ravenala is called "the traveler's tree" because a thirsty traveler can break off the lower end of a leaf stem and find a small supply of water. The tropical rain-forests of the east coast contain valuable hardwood trees, along with groves of mangoes, coconuts, and bananas. The most familiar tree on the western plains is the oddly shaped baobab, which holds water in its trunk. Madagascar boasts six species of the tree, while Africa has only one. Octopus trees, which resemble cacti, thrive in the south, and ferns and bamboo trees flourish in the highlands.

Some of Madagascar's unusual plants have important medicinal or economic applications. The island's periwinkles, for example, contain an extract that is used in drugs that treat leukemia (a blood disease). The katrafay, when soaked in bathwater, can relieve muscular pain, and the kily's bark soothes rheumatism and measles. Pods from vanilla orchid vines provide the raw material for vanilla extract, one of the country's major export items.

FAUNA

Like its plant life, Madagascar's animals are unusual and, in many cases, unique to the island. One of the most interesting native creatures is the lemur. At least 39

Courtesy of Philip Allen

Southern areas of Madagascar, which receive little rainfall, support desert vegetation, such as cacti.

Courtesy of American Lutheran Church

With its warm climate, Madagascar supports many flowering plants. The red blossoms of this woody vine, called a bougain-villea, ornament a porch in Antananarivo.

Malagasy farmers—in need of pasture and farmland—have stripped much of the highlands of vegetation. A reforestation plan aims to replace at least some of the lost trees.

species and subspecies have been identified. Most lemurs are found only in Madagascar, but a few relatives exist in Africa and Asia. The gray, short-tailed babacoote is the largest Madagascar lemur. The aye-aye, another family member, only comes out of hiding at night. The most common lemur, and one that can be tamed, is the maki. Although lemurs are protected by law, many are hunted illegally for food.

Madagascar also contains half of the world's chameleons—small lizards that can change color and that can move one eye independently of the other. Fully half of the

Twilight reveals the thick trunks and spindly branches of a sparse grove of baobabs in southern Madagascar. These unusual trees hold moisture in reserve for times of drought.

Photo by Alton Halverson

Madagascar's lemurs, such as these members of the ring-tailed species, usually walk on all fours and are most active at night. (Lemur comes from the Latin word for nighttime spirits.) These gentle animals feed on insects, leaves, birds' eggs, and small reptiles.

island's birds—including ground rollers, courols, mesites, and vangas—and nearly all of its mammals are found only in Madagascar.

Resident in the island's ocean waters are a small number of coelacanths—large, blue-scaled fish. Scientists believed that the fish was extinct until fishermen caught one in the Mozambique Channel in the mid-twentieth century. This species of fish first appeared 350 million years ago.

Hunting by humans has caused the extinction on Madagascar of the pygmy hippopotamus, a dozen varieties of lemurs, and the giant tortoise. Little of the national budget is devoted to conservation, and scientists believe that more of Madagascar's unique wildlife and plants are in serious danger of being destroyed.

Ibis inhabit the swampy coastal areas of Madagascar, eating fish and reptiles for nourishment and building nests in weeds or bushes.

Independent Picture Service

Cities

Over 20 percent of the Malagasy live in urban areas, which are sprinkled throughout the island. Migration to metropolitan areas has pressured the cities to provide jobs, housing, and services. The densest populations are located on the east coast and in the middle zone of the Central Highlands.

Antananarivo (population one million), the capital of Madagascar, is situated in the highlands, halfway between the northern and southern coasts. In the Malagasy language, the name means "Town of a Thousand" and dates from the early seventeenth century, when a Merina king stationed a garrison of 1,000 men on the site.

The capital is a city of contrasts, with broad avenues, winding lanes, modern buildings, and ancient palaces. Automobiles compete for road space with zebu-hauled, two-wheeled carts. A newly developed area in the center of the city boasts apartment houses, a large hospital, and many government buildings. Only a short distance away are rice fields and small farm dwellings. On top of a hill overlooking the city stand the palaces of former kings, queens, prime ministers, and presidents of Madagascar.

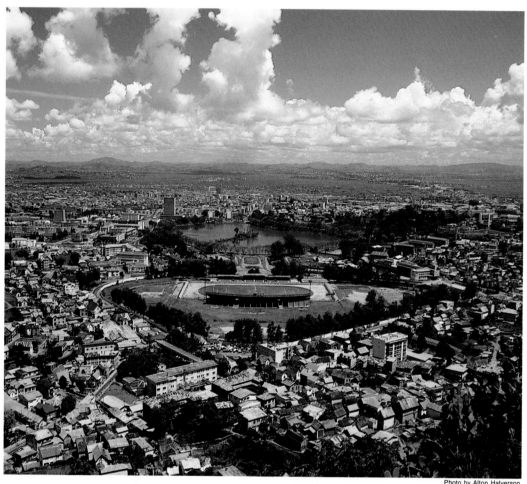

Photo by Alton Halverson

Lying in a valley within the Ankaratra Massif (mountain range), Antananarivo is Madagascar's largest city. Lake Anosy is in the center of the metropolis, surrounded by jacaranda trees.

A flower market in the capital displays the variety of the island's vegetation.

Rows of two-story brick houses arranged in tiers hug the hillsides surrounding Antananarivo.

In downtown areas of the capital, rickshas are still used to transport goods—in this case an assortment of empty bottles.

Another large inland city is Fianarantsoa, with a population of 80,000. Located 250 miles south of Antananarivo in the heart of a large farming area, this city is the main urban center of the south. The main inhabitants of this area are the Betsileo, who are experts in the irrigation and cultivation of terraced rice fields. The name Fianarantsoa means "The Place of Good Learning."

Toamasina is the most important city along the east coast. With a population of 90,000, it is the main port of the island and has road, rail, and air connections to the capital. Toamasina has a large petroleum refinery and is also the point of export for important agricultural products, such as coffee, bananas, cloves, and vanilla.

The major seaport on the northwestern coast is Mahajanga, a city of 85,000 people situated at the mouth of the Betsiboka River. Tons of brick-red soil from the highlands are washed into the waters of nearby Bombetoka Bay from the river so that large ships must anchor offshore.

At the extreme northern tip of Madagascar is the port city of Antsiranana, with a population of 60,000. In addition to

Courtesy of Philip Allen

Once called Diégo-Suarez, Antsiranana has a mixed cultural heritage resulting from its position at the northernmost tip of Madagascar—a region accessible to African, European, and Asian ships.

exporting peanuts and coffee, the city has a large, deepwater bay that the French used as a naval base earlier in the twentieth century.

Independent Picture Service

Freighters crowd the port of Toamasina, a well-developed harbor that exports the island's cloves, vanilla, and coffee.

Photo by Alton Halverson

Beginning in about the fifth century A.D., Madagascar's peaceful waters and beautiful scenery welcomed early migrations of people from Southeast Asia.

2) History and Government

Little is known about the early history of Madagascar. Malayo-Polynesian migrations, which formed the cultural roots of the Malagasy, probably began in the fifth century A.D. and ended before the thirteenth century. Traveling in large canoes, the original settlers came from the Malay Archipelago—a group of islands located about 4,000 miles east of Madagascar—after spending time in southern Asia and East Africa. Some of the newcomers moved up to the Central Highlands, where the climate was mild and where good land was plentiful.

Along the coasts, the early Malagasy traded with peoples from Africa and the Comoro Islands. Arab traders arrived after the founding of the Islamic religion in the seventh century A.D. as part of an effort to conquer and establish communities. Arab settlements developed on both the west and east coasts beginning in the ninth century, and Arab traders provided the first written accounts of the island. By the tenth century the Arabs successfully controlled most of the trade in the western half of the Indian Ocean.

Early Times

Beginning in the sixteenth century, several important kingdoms developed in different parts of Madagascar. Among them were the Anteimoro kingdom of the southeast and the Sakalava kingdoms of the northwest and southwest. Most of the

19

island's political units were very loosely organized into a system that included nobles, free people, and slaves. These realms tended to break up into small areas, so that the island was dotted with a mosaic of chiefdoms and kingdoms by the eighteenth century.

An exception to this general pattern was the Merina state. In part because of its isolation in the Central Highlands, the kingdom grew strong and was able to absorb smaller, surrounding groups.

The Arrival of the Europeans

After explorations of the island by the Portuguese captain Diégo Dias in 1500, the Portuguese tried to establish a settlement on the southeastern coast. Between 1528 and 1618, they made several attempts to colonize Madagascar. All of the efforts failed, and they never returned to the island, which they had named São Lourenço (Saint Lawrence). Legend relates that the thirteenth-century Italian explorer Marco Polo was the first person to dub the island Madagascar—a region he had heard of, but had not visited, on his travels to Asia.

The next Europeans to venture to Madagascar were French sailors from Dieppe, who exchanged weapons for supplies of food and water. Dutch navigators also traveled to the island for similar purposes. In the early seventeenth century royal support from the French king Louis XIV helped to establish small settlements on Madagascar at Fort Dauphin (modern Tolagnaro) and Cape Sainte-Marie. But the newcomers were either killed or driven off by the Malagasy, or they succumbed to local diseases.

At about the same time, British captains began to make regular stops at Madagascar to restock their ships. At first, the local peoples fled into the forests as soon as the British vessels appeared. In time, however, the Malagasy grew used to the arrival and departure of the visitors, and

Early settlers hunted the island's abundant wildlife.

In the sixteenth century Portuguese crews sailed their ships into Madagascar's bays to establish colonial settlements and to search for people to enslave.

trade between the British and the islanders eventually became routine.

Piracy and Slavery

No strong naval power patrolled the area, so the western Indian Ocean became popular among French and British pirates in the late seventeenth and early eighteenth centuries. The pirates plundered vessels from many nations and used the east coast of Madagascar as a headquarters for their operations. They established friendly relations with the Malagasy, and some of the pirates settled permanently on the island, becoming influential in local communities. When British naval activity increased in the Indian Ocean, piracy gradually died out.

Slavery had become well established among the peoples of Madagascar by the eighteenth century. Fighting between rival clans produced prisoners of war who were eventually enslaved, and slave populations increased through both raids and the birth of children to slave women. Slave trading flourished, and many shipwrecked sailors and pirates ended up as laborers to Malagasy rulers. Most captives were sent to nearby islands; some were even exported to the New World.

The Merina Kingdom

Throughout the period of European arrivals and departures, internal strife existed among the many kingdoms on the island. The Betsileo established a small domain in the center, and the Sakalava formed two large kingdoms—the Menabe and Boina—in the west. At one time, Sakalava influence spread over half of the island. From one of the realm's smaller states in the Central Highlands the Merina kingdom

The design of this colorful Christian tomb combines Malagasy customs with the Christian beliefs brought to the island from Europe.

King Radama I ruled the Merina kingdom from 1810 to 1828. His rule was marked by attempts to modernize the realm and to establish trade agreements with European nations.

Ranavalona, the wife of Radama I, governed the Merina lands from the time of her husband's death in 1828 until 1861. She strongly disagreed with Radama's pro-Western stance and rejected contacts with Europe.

developed, and it controlled almost the entire island through much of the nineteenth century.

The Merina had been divided into four branches until the end of the eighteenth century, when one of the leaders, Andrianampoinimerina, united the four subgroups. The aim of King Andrianampoinimerina was to unify Madagascar. Although his rule was harsh, he established law and order, redistributed land, and controlled water resources for irrigation.

Radama I

Upon the death of Andrianampoinimerina, his son Radama succeeded to the Merina throne in 1810. An able and far-seeing administrator, Radama I modernized the army and extended his kingdom to the eastern and southern coasts.

Partially to stabilize his new lands, the king welcomed the help and technology of the British and the French. In exchange for firearms, manufactured goods, and military training, Radama permitted the British and French to establish trading posts. He also allowed them to send Christian missionaries as advisers to the capital and to use some of the island's vacant land to establish plantations. The London Missionary Society began teaching at Antananarivo, and a generation of Malagasy nobles learned the English language. A printing office published books and pamphlets, including fragments of the Bible and a few school textbooks, in English and in Malagasy.

Under a treaty with Sir Robert Farquhar, governor of the British-held island of Mauritius, Radama obtained military aid. In exchange, the king pledged to abolish the export of slaves—a practice that had been making many of his nobles rich.

The French also were allowed to teach Merina aristocrats and to trade along the east coast. But they lost favor with the king by befriending Radama's Sakalava rivals on the western and northern coasts.

Ranavalona I

Radama I died in 1828 at the age of 36. During his reign, he had unified most of the island and had brought it to international standing. The crown passed to Radama's first wife, Ranavalona I, who strongly distrusted the Europeans. The queen believed that missionaries, merchants, and plantation operators posed a threat to Malagasy authority. Consequently, her government made the Christian religion illegal and ordered the deaths of thousands of Malagasy Christians. Many others were imprisoned or enslaved. For a time, Ranavalona's policies excluded all Europeans from Antananarivo, and foreign commerce nearly ceased.

Most Europeans fled the island, but one of the few who remained—a Frenchman named Jean Laborde—secured the trust of the queen. Laborde brought some technological advancement to the island. With enslaved laborers at his disposal, Laborde produced arms, textiles, paper, pottery, soap, ink, and sugar. With the queen's support, he was able to introduce new vegetation to the island and to improve its cattle breeds.

As long as Laborde did not import European political ideas, he had the queen's trust and support. She even allowed Laborde to help educate her son and heir, who thus developed a favorable view of France. Eventually, however, plots to overthrow Ranavalona caused her to temporarily deport Laborde, along with all other foreigners, in 1858.

Soldiers, servants, and officials of the traditional Merina faith accompanied Ranavalona I on her public appearances.

A martyrs' grave commemorates Christians who died under Ranavalona's rule because they would not give up their religion.

Courtesy of American Lutheran Church

A palace rebellion in 1863 removed the European-influenced king Radama II *(right)* after only a year on the Merina throne. After Radama's death, his wife Rasoherina *(far right)* eventually married her prime minister, and her five-year rule saw a rise in the number of Christian missionaries on the island.

Independent Picture Service

Independent Picture Service

24

The harshness of Ranavalona's rule caused frequent uprisings, which—coupled with the queen's desire to expand Merina holdings—brought war and destruction to distant provinces. In 1841 French troops agreed to protect two Sakalava leaders in the northwestern area from the Merina. In this way, the French gained control of the small islands of Noissi-Bé and Sainte-Marie, which became the first successful French footholds near the mainland.

The queen reintroduced slavery as punishment for a wide range of crimes, and this revived both internal and external slave markets. Great numbers of African slaves from the nearby eastern coast of the continent were brought in to fill Malagasy slave labor needs that could not be met locally. The slave trade was thus resumed, arousing British opposition to Ranavalona's policies.

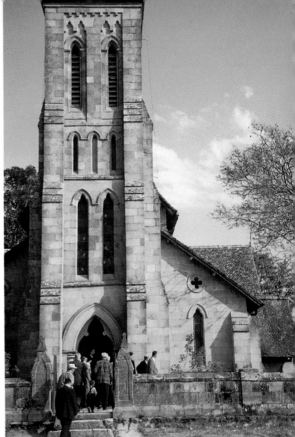

As a result of the government's liberal policy toward missionaries, Christian churches were built in Antananarivo and throughout the kingdom.

The Last Merina Monarchs

When Ranavalona's son, Radama II, came to the throne after his mother's death in 1861, European influence returned. Catholic missionaries came to the island and reopened schools and churches. Radama II's regime abolished punishment by death and released religious and political prisoners. But the king's European and Malagasy companions dominated his decisions. Fearing the overpowering influence of the Europeans, some of Radama's counselors organized a palace revolution in 1863. During the coup d'état, the king was strangled to death.

The last three Merina monarchs—Rasoherina, Ranavalona II, and Ranavalona III—were women, and each married the same prime minister, Rainilaiarivony, during her reign. In this way Rainilaiarivony

Using his position as husband of the last three Merina queens, Rainilaiarivony was able to influence national decisions and public policy for three decades.

European influence eventually appeared in the architecture of local Malagasy buildings, which took on a distinctly French style.

strongly influenced Madagascar's political affairs for 31 years.

Following Radama II's death, his wife, Rasoherina, ruled. She reinstated punishment by death and restored customs duties. The new queen signed treaties with the governments of Britain, France, and the United States. As a result, more Christian groups—including Roman Catholics, Anglicans, Quakers, and Lutherans—came to Madagascar. The missionaries opened hospitals and dispensaries, and the success of a Scottish physician in conquering a smallpox epidemic further increased European influence.

Rasoherina was succeeded by her cousin, Ramona, who reigned under the name Ranavalona II. One of the new queen's first acts was to recognize Christianity publicly. She and her husband, Rainilaiarivony, were baptized in a Protestant ceremony. In 1869 the government ordered the destruction of sacred idols—religious symbols of traditional Malagasy beliefs.

Ranavalona II, who succeeded her cousin Rasoherina in 1868, ordered traditional Malagasy sacred idols to be destroyed to show her public acceptance of Christianity.

26

The Merina ruled the central part of the island directly. The kingdoms of the east and northeast were dependent, but the south and part of the west remained independent. Merina rule satisfied British commercial and cultural interests but was not satisfactory to the French.

France attempted to weaken Merina authority in the north and west by claiming land there for settlers from the French-held island of Réunion. French claims were based on treaties made with local leaders of the region in the 1840s.

British and French rivalry continued until the early 1880s, when Britain and France—along with several other European nations—agreed to recognize one another's colonial territories in and near Africa. As a result, France left Egypt to the British in exchange for more power in Madagascar.

Wars Between Madagascar and France

Queen Ranavalona II died of pneumonia in July 1883, and her niece, Ranavalona

Queen Ranavalona III, the last Merina ruler, refused to recognize French land claims on the island. Her stance led to wars that eventually caused her kingdom to come under direct French control.

Merina monarchs lived in a large palace, originally built for Ranavalona I, that still stands on a hill high above Antananarivo.

The capital's expansion and development dates from the late nineteenth century, when a French colonial administration took over the island.

III, succeeded her. The new queen refused to recognize French claims in the north-western part of the island. As a result, war broke out between the French and the Merina kingdom. The Merina were defeated, and, after long negotiations, a treaty was signed on December 17, 1885. Provisions of the treaty declared that the foreign relations of Madagascar would be directed by a French resident-general and that Diégo-Suarez Bay (now Antsiranana Bay) and the surrounding territory would be given to France.

The Merina postponed complete French domination by keeping in close contact with the British. In 1890, in return for French concessions in Zanzibar, the British government agreed to recognize Madagascar as a French protectorate, which was declared in 1894. Rainilaiarivony, however, continued to arm and train a domestic army with the help of the British. This activity caused the French government to demand Madagascar's compliance with the 1885 treaty.

Madagascar did not comply, and war broke out again at the end of 1894. Malagasy soldiers fought the French invading army through most of 1895, but the French troops reached Antananarivo on September 30. The next day, the French commander in charge of the expedition, General Duchesne, signed a treaty with the queen's representatives that recognized French control over Madagascar.

French Rule

In 1896, after revolts in various parts of the island, the French legislature passed a law making Madagascar a French colony. All slaves on the island were set free, and General Joseph-Simon Gallieni arrived from France to take over civil and military command of the island.

One of General Gallieni's early acts was to abolish the monarchy. He exiled Queen Ranavalona III, and she died in Algeria in 1917. The once-powerful prime minister Rainilaiarivony was also sent away. By

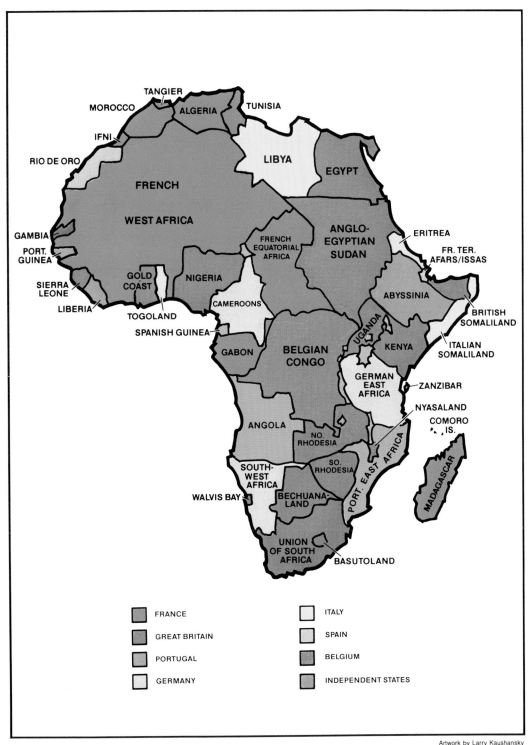

TANGIER

MOROCCO
ALGERIA
TUNISIA

IFNI

RIO DE ORO

LIBYA

EGYPT

FRENCH

WEST AFRICA

GAMBIA

PORT.
GUINEA

SIERRA
LEONE

LIBERIA

GOLD
COAST

NIGERIA

TOGOLAND

SPANISH GUINEA

FRENCH
EQUATORIAL
AFRICA

CAMEROONS

GABON

ANGLO-
EGYPTIAN
SUDAN

ERITREA

FR. TER.
AFARS/ISSAS

ABYSSINIA

BRITISH
SOMALILAND

ITALIAN
SOMALILAND

BELGIAN
CONGO

UGANDA

KENYA

GERMAN
EAST
AFRICA

ZANZIBAR

NYASALAND

COMORO
IS.

ANGOLA

NO.
RHODESIA

SO.
RHODESIA

PORT. EAST AFRICA

MADAGASCAR

SOUTH-
WEST
AFRICA

WALVIS BAY

BECHUANA-
LAND

UNION
OF SOUTH
AFRICA

BASUTOLAND

	FRANCE		ITALY
	GREAT BRITAIN		SPAIN
	PORTUGAL		BELGIUM
	GERMANY		INDEPENDENT STATES

Artwork by Larry Kaushansky

During the European scramble for African colonies that occurred in the last decades of the 1800s, France made Madagascar a protectorate and added the island to its widespread colonial holdings on the continent. Map information taken from *The Anchor Atlas of World History*, 1978.

1898 the authority of France had been established throughout the island. Gallieni set up a colonial administration and divided the country into provinces, districts, and cantons.

The colonial administration built roads and better port facilities and extended postal and telegraph services. During this period, improvements in educational and health standards, including the control of several preventable epidemic diseases, also occurred. French and Roman Catholic traditions were introduced, and Madagascar's economy became closely tied to that of France. Government grants of land to French colonists from Réunion and commercial rights to French companies, however, were not welcome developments to the Malagasy.

Opposition to Colonial Rule

Opposition to French colonial authority emerged several times. The earliest peoples to oppose French rule were groups to the south who refused to surrender after the island's war with France ended in 1895. But these peoples also felt a strong resentment toward the deposed Merina, who had adopted European ways.

The first nationalist stirrings arose among Western-educated members of the Merina. Their secret society—Vy Vato Sakelika (VVS)—reacted to the failure of the French to develop a prosperous economy, and they resented the privileges that were granted to colonists from Réunion. The VVS was discovered, and the colonial government either imprisoned or deported the society's members.

Courtesy of Philip Allen

A war memorial to Malagasy soldiers who participated in World War I stands in front of a Lutheran church in Ampanihy, southern Madagascar.

Watched by a young Malagasy child, a South African soldier guards his post. In order to prevent Japanese soldiers from crossing the Indian Ocean to take Madagascar during World War II, British and South African troops occupied the island.

Photo by Library of Congress

Malagasy troops had served during World War I, and veterans of that war became a second source of nationalist agitation. Many ex-soldiers remained in France in the 1920s and 1930s, absorbing liberal French ideas. The French League for Madagascar formed at this time and demanded full French citizenship for all Malagasy people.

A young Betsileo teacher, Jean Ralaimongo, joined the French League and returned to the island. With other nationalists, he organized a strike in Antananarivo in 1929. Several of the strike leaders were arrested; others, including Ralaimongo, were forbidden to leave their houses. Thereafter, the nationalists promoted the idea of Madagascar's independence from France.

During World War II, basic survival became more important to the Malagasy than nationalist sentiments. France fell in 1940, and in 1942 British and South African forces occupied the island to keep Japanese submarines away until Madagascar came under the authority of the Free French (a group opposed to the German-controlled government in France) in 1943.

Dignitaries arrive in Antananarivo to attend celebrations in honor of Madagascar's independence day—June 26, 1960.

Veterans of the war, mostly from the Merina, formed the Democratic Movement for Malagasy Revival (MDRM). The basis of their political platform was to gain immediate independence for Madagascar within the French Union. In 1946 three MDRM members won election to the French legislature in Paris. Their petitions for self-government in Madagascar were rejected, and on March 29, 1947, revolts broke out in several parts of the island, especially in the east. The uprisings caused 80,000 to 100,000 deaths. The Malagasy deputies and the MDRM were blamed for

When the country was still named the Malagasy Republic, it issued airmail stamps that featured a pair of lemurs and that declared the nation's intention to protect its wildlife (*la faune*).

the rebellion, which lasted well into 1948. The colonial government exiled the leaders, crushing the MDRM politically.

Nationalists faced severe repression for another decade, but local hopes for independence remained active, especially among the Merina and among smaller ethnic groups, which had traditionally been without power. Although Malagasy disillusionment with the French continued, the colonial administration remained in control of the island until 1958, when the regime of Charles de Gaulle came to power.

The Malagasy Republic

In keeping with the new colonial policy of self-government for French overseas territories, Madagascar voted to become a self-governing republic within the French Community on October 14, 1958. This relationship with France was short-lived, however. On June 26, 1960, Madagascar

Philibert Tsiranana became the first president of the Malagasy Republic on May 1, 1959. About a year later, Madagascar declared its full independence and withdrew from the French Community.

Charles de Gaulle developed the idea of the French Community, which joined independent French territories — including Madagascar — in a voluntary federation with France.

became the fully independent Malagasy Republic. Through technical assistance and advisers, France continued to exert considerable influence over the nation.

The republic's first president, Philibert Tsiranana, was head of the Social Democratic party (PSD). Although the party had tried to absorb the strongest nationalist elements in the country, Tsiranana announced that he would pursue close ties with France. The government's moderate economic policies were aimed at stabilizing the nation and bringing long-sought social benefits, such as health care and education, to more of the population. Despite this goal, a wide gap still existed between the Merina elite and the rest of the country.

On March 30, 1965, a huge majority of voters elected President Tsiranana to a

General Gabriel Ramanantsoa took over the government in 1972 and nationalized (changed from private to government ownership) many farms and foreign-owned businesses.

Among the problems Malagasy regimes face is widespread disease. This mother and child suffer from illnesses associated with poor nutrition and unsafe water.

second term. The Social Democrats retained their firm alliance with Europe and the United States, but the Independent Congress party (AKFM), which controlled city government in the capital, demanded more contacts with the Soviet Union and Asia. Members of the National Independence movement (MONIMA), who wanted a complete break with France, also opposed the PSD.

The government brought neither stability nor prosperity, and the PSD became corrupt and internally divided. Nevertheless, President Tsiranana was elected to a third term in March of 1972. Throughout 1971 and 1972, however, students had gone on strike to demand educational reforms and economic independence from France. The student movement gained wide support and soon became national. In May the strikes turned into riots, and urban poor people, who demanded more fundamental economic changes, joined the student demonstrators. On May 18, 1972, President Tsiranana resigned and gave General Gabriel Ramanantsoa the authority to organize a new government.

One of Madagascar's long-standing concerns is its inability to produce enough food to feed its population. Here, a farmer walks through a field of rice—a staple crop that still needs to be imported to satisfy demand.

34

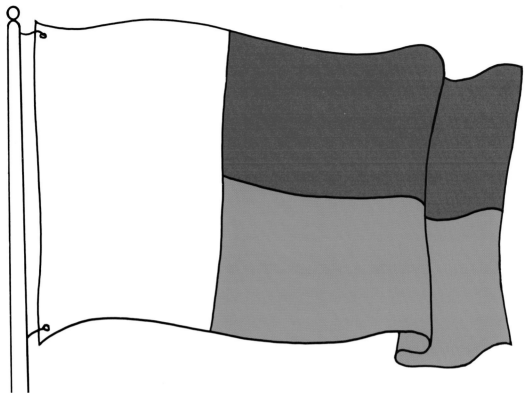

The Malagasy flag was adopted in 1959, and its colors were originally associated with prominent island peoples. White has come to symbolize purity of ideals, red to stand for independence, and green to represent coastal inhabitants.

The Second Republic

General Ramanantsoa formed a military government of austerity and reform. He reduced Madagascar's ties with France and broke all contacts with South Africa, whose policy of apartheid—racial separateness—was unacceptable to the Malagasy. The regime sought to invest power in the traditional village councils, called *fokonolona.*

But the regime could not hold the country together against pressure from both radicals and conservatives. It collapsed in early 1975, and, by the end of that year, Didier Ratsiraka had been installed as president of a revolutionary second republic. The new regime sought to form a strict, socialist government that would address some of Madagascar's long-standing social and economic problems.

Although Didier Ratsiraka *(left)* strengthened Madagascar's ties with the Soviet Union, he also made contacts with Western powers and has tried to remain free of excessive foreign influence.

Since taking power, Ratsiraka's goal has been to achieve a one-party state. Six parties exist, and all are members of the government's National Democratic Revolutionary Front. Old parties, like AKFM, MONIMA, and other leftist factions, are balanced somewhat by Christian Democrats, Social Democrats, and the president's party—the Revolutionary Advance Guard (AREMA).

In 1983 AREMA won 117 of the 137 seats in the national legislature, as well as over 90 percent of the local and district offices. Opposition to Ratsiraka comes mainly from the uncompromising nationalists in MONIMA, whose leader, Monja Jaona, has become a symbol of resistance. Never-theless, Ratsiraka was reelected in 1982 and in 1989 to additional seven-year terms.

The 1980s

France and the European Economic Community are still important to Madagascar in economic affairs, but the island is active in the Third World and among socialist states. Madagascar is a strong advocate of nonalignment (a neutral political stand that favors neither the East nor the West), disarmament (reduced weaponry and armed forces), and a demilitarized zone of peace in the Indian Ocean.

Economic hardships and ethnic hostilities among the islanders characterized

Among other reforms, the Ratsiraka regime has removed the price controls on rice, allowing farmers to sell it at market value. The government hopes the new approach will increase the amount of rice grown by the nation's farmers.

A young girl in Antananarivo presents a gift to Pope John Paul II during his visit to Madagascar in April 1989. Thousands of Malagasy attended religious services that the Pope conducted in several cities.

Madagascar in the mid-1980s. In 1986 President Ratsiraka changed the island's economic focus toward projects that would attract private investments and Western currency. For example, he encouraged foreign investments by lowering taxes and discounting import duties.

Rice farmers are permitted to sell their product at market prices rather than at amounts imposed by the government. The switch from pure socialism to a system that in some ways resembles a market-oriented economy has caused further political dissent.

Government

In theory, Madagascar is decentralized into over 11,000 village councils (fokonolona). In practice, however, the national government makes all the large-scale decisions. President Ratsiraka's book, *Charter of the Malagasy Socialist Revolution,* guides all decision making, and only people who accept the book's ideas are allowed to run for election.

The regime is dedicated to abolishing privileged classes—that is, to making all citizens equal in terms of wealth and opportunity. The authority to achieve this goal belongs to the president, who is advised by a 20-member revolutionary council and by a national assembly. The president appoints the council, maintaining a balance between civilians and military personnel and between conservatives and radicals. The assembly's 137 members are directly elected, but they cannot enact legislation against the president's will.

A prime minister and cabinet are appointed by the president to carry out the president's laws and policies. The judicial system remains loosely structured on the French model, but procedures have been simplified, and people's courts occasionally decide judicial questions. For administrative purposes, Madagascar is divided into six provinces.

Antananarivo's main market, called the Zoma (meaning "Friday" in Malagasy), is held daily. On Fridays, however, the number of stalls increases, filling most of the town center.

3) The People

Although Madagascar is often considered to be part of Africa, the Malagasy people are not Africans. They represent a mixture of Indonesians, Africans, and other ethnic groups. The family unit—which includes grandparents, uncles, aunts, nephews, nieces, and countless cousins—is of extreme importance in Malagasy life.

The population of Madagascar numbers 11.6 million. Of this amount, approximately 100,000 are non-Malagasy, including 20,000 French people, 15,000 East Indians, and 10,000 Chinese. In recent years, the population has been increasing at the rate of 3.1 percent a year. This rate of growth may double the number of Mala-

gasy in 22 years. In addition, 44 percent of the population are under the age of 15, and 3 percent are over the age of 65. These high population indicators put more pressure on Madagascar's land and other natural and economic resources.

Ethnic Groups

Although the Malagasy form one nation with one language and culture, 18 different ethnic groups have been identified. The largest group is the Merina, with an approximate population of two million. The Merina live in the Central Highlands. Indeed, their name means "people of the highlands." Mostly of Malayo-Polynesian ancestry, the Merina vary in appearance from light-skinned to very dark.

At one time, the Merina were divided into three castes—nobles, free people, and slaves. Although these designations have long been abolished, the caste system still influences Merina society. Forming the ruling class before the French took control of the island, some members of the group today grow rice and herd cattle. Urbanized Merina make up the largest educated class.

The Betsimisaraka, meaning "the many inseparables," number well over one million and live mainly on the east coast in the Toamasina area. The second largest ethnic group in Madagascar, the Betsimisaraka have absorbed immigrants from southern Asia, Indonesia, and Arab nations. For the most part, they live by cultivating rice, by fishing, or by working on plantations in the region.

The third largest group, the Betsileo (meaning "the many invincibles") populate

Courtesy of Philip Allen

A Betsileo *mpilalao*, or musical troupe, entertains a crowd in a village of south central Madagascar.

Courtesy of American Lutheran Church

The traditional structure of some ethnic groups still exists. Here, the local leader, or chief, of the Mahafaly people of southwestern Madagascar holds a symbol of his authority.

the southern part of the Central Highlands near Fianarantsoa. The Betsileo number about one million and are experts in irrigating and cultivating sloped rice fields. Along with the Merina, the Betsileo have a rather privileged position in Malagasy society and hold many skilled and professional positions.

The Tsimihety, or "those who do not cut their hair," derived their name centuries ago when, in order to show their independence, they refused to cut their hair—a traditional sign of mourning—when a Sakalava king died. Although the Tsimihety

Independent Picture Service

Among the many cultural traditions of the Malagasy are the African-influenced hairstyles that feature tightly braided strands in symmetric patterns.

DISTRIBUTION OF ETHNIC GROUPS

ANTAKARANA
BETSIMISARAKA
TSIMIHETY
MAKOA
SAKALAVA
SIHANAKA
BEZANOZANO
BETSIMISARAKA
MERINA
SAKALAVA
BETSILEO
TANALA
ANTAMBAHOAKA
BARA
ANTAIMORO
ANTAIFASY
ANTAISAKA
MAKOA
MAHAFALY
ANTANOSY
ANTANOSY
ANTANDROY

Independent Picture Service

Although internal migrations of Madagascar's ethnic groups occur, this drawing indicates their general locations on the island.

live principally in the north central area, they have a reputation for frequently migrating and settling new or neighboring lands. They are the fourth largest ethnic group in Madagascar, with a population of about 650,000.

Although the Sakalava, who number 500,000, live closest to Africa, they have strong Asian influences in their physical and cultural characteristics. Their lands stretch over a long strip between Toliary and Mahajanga, and their name means "people of the long valleys." Once members of the largest and most powerful kingdom on Madagascar, they are now a cattle-raising people. Their territory is still the most extensive on the island, but the Tsimihety have recently moved into the region as well.

Language and Communications

The two official languages in Madagascar are Malagasy and French. All of the

Traditional Merina storyteller-musicians perform in the Central Highlands, wearing the lambas (shawls) and redingotes (fitted coats) that identify their profession.

A dancer and several musicians entertain children in a Tsimihety village of northern Madagascar.

Interested customers browse in a religious bookstore, where the merchandise is published in both Malagasy and French.

islanders speak dialects of Malagasy, which is used in elementary and secondary schools. French is returning to prominence in education, however, and is commonly employed in international affairs. But outside the cities and government offices, few Malagasy speak French well.

Malagasy is of Malayo-Polynesian origin. Over the centuries various tongues were brought from other lands. These contributions, as well as Malagasy's isolation from its spoken roots in southeastern Asia, have produced a language in its own right. Its 21-letter alphabet is written in upright type (as is English), and its words contain many syllables and are rich in poetic images. For example, the English word, "sun," in Malagasy is *masoandro,* which literally means "eye of the day."

In addition to the symbolic ideas of everyday speech, family names also have meanings. *Ra,* found at the beginning of a great number of names, is a prefix of respect, much like the use of "Mr." For example, a young boy might be called Ikoto, but when he is grown up, he will be Rakoto.

The government controls radio, television, and numerous publications, including sources of official government information. Many newspapers are published in the capital, but some are only a single sheet with a very small readership. The largest paper is the *Madagascar Matin,* written mainly in French; the rest of the press publishes in Malagasy. Although politics are vigorously discussed by Malagasy newspaper readers, press censorship prevails.

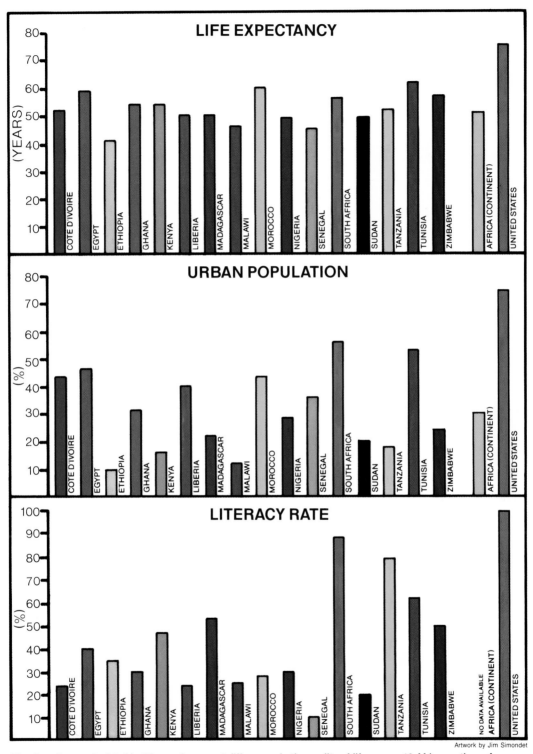

LIFE EXPECTANCY

URBAN POPULATION

LITERACY RATE

Artwork by Jim Simondet

The three factors depicted in this graph suggest differences in the quality of life among 16 African nations. Averages for the United States and the entire continent of Africa are included for comparison. Data taken from "1987 World Population Data Sheet" and *PC-Globe*.

Carrying their books, rural children leave their village to attend a local primary school.

Education

Until recently, only half of the young people in Madagascar went to school, and most of them did not go beyond the elementary grades. About 11 percent of those attending school went on to some form of secondary education. In the 1980s over 100 academic and technical high schools existed on the island. The University of Antananarivo opened in 1961, and the government has founded universities in all six of the provincial capitals. The total number of university students is estimated to be about 30,000. Soviet and East

In the 1980s a high percentage of Malagasy youth attended secondary-school classes, such as this one at a Lutheran high school in the southwestern town of Bezaha.

Villagers gather to collect safe drinking water at a newly installed pump. About 9 percent of rural people and 73 percent of the urban population have access to sources of pure water.

European teachers sent to Madagascar usually require interpreters to help them teach their courses.

Throughout the country, about 60 percent of the men can read and write, whereas this is true of only 40 percent of the women. The revolutionary government broke away from the French system of education and introduced a new procedure better adapted to the particular needs and goals of the Malagasy nation. This move aimed to give equal opportunity to all, with special provision for children in poorer families. Some complain, however, that Malagasy education has fallen in quality and that students should be taught in French.

Health

Medical services include 10 hospitals and 300 medical clinics. Tuberculosis and leprosy pose serious health problems, but an organized fight against disease has wiped out nearly all cases of bubonic plague and has reduced the prevalence of malaria.

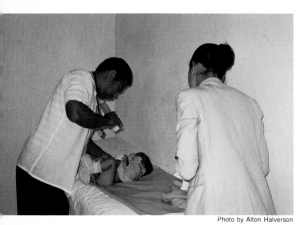

Photo by Alton Halverson

As its concerned mother looks on, a Malagasy baby is examined in a Lutheran medical clinic.

The infant mortality rate is 110 deaths in every 1,000 live births—a figure that is almost as high as the rate for East Africa. Life expectancy is 53 years, which is average for the African continent as a whole. Nevertheless, only one-quarter of the population has access to safe drinking water.

To some degree, health problems are related to the limited amount of food and to the unvaried diet of many Malagasy. Efforts to increase the production of rice and to introduce new foods—such as fish—for domestic consumption may help to raise nutritional standards on the island.

Courtesy of Philip Allen

This traditional Malagasy structure is a memorial to a Christian family of southern Madagascar.

Although Madagascar's population of Muslims (followers of Islam) is relatively small, mosques, or Islamic houses of worship, exist in urban centers throughout the island. This mosque is located in Toliary, southwestern Madagascar.

Photo by Alton Halverson

Special tombs mark the graves of Malagasy who supported traditional beliefs. The sites display *aloala,* or symbolic carvings, as well as cattle horns.

Religion

Religion plays a role in all aspects of Malagasy life. Coexisting with organized Western and Eastern religious beliefs is a complex group of traditional customs and prohibitions (called *fady*) that emphasize the vitality of the entire universe. Religion in Madagascar is based on the ideas that the world has meaning, that human life has purpose, and that personal actions are important. This traditional religious attitude also includes a strong reverence for a person's ancestors.

ISLAM AND CHRISTIANITY

The first organized foreign religion to affect Madagascar was Islam, which was founded by the prophet Muhammad in what is now Saudi Arabia in the seventh century A.D. Arab traders brought Islam to Madagascar in the ninth century. Today about 80,000 Muslims (followers of Islam) live in Madagascar.

The London Missionary Society introduced Christianity to the island in about 1818. British missionaries were followed by Catholics, Anglicans, Lutherans, and Quakers from other countries. These various religious groups had a noticeable effect on the history and social development of the country. They established schools and churches, and today about one-third of the Malagasy are Christians; nearly half of these are Roman Catholics. Pope John Paul II visited Madagascar in April 1989. He urged the people to struggle against the poverty that threatens their nation.

TRADITIONAL BELIEFS

Long before Christianity was introduced to the country, the Malagasy believed in Andriamanitra, the supreme creator. It is the *razana* (ancestors), however, who show the Malagasy how to live their lives. For Malagasy believers, death does not mean that a person has left the family. The dead are thought to have enormous influence, and those left behind must do everything they can to avoid being disrespectful to the memory of deceased relations.

The Malagasy's belief in eternal life centers around the family tomb, and the worst thing that could happen to a Malagasy is not to be buried with the family. Specific occasions—such as the beginning of a harvest, a wedding, a burial, or the building of a new home—require special gifts to the dead.

This *mpanandro,* or seer, of the Bara people holds a small *valiha* (a musical instrument) and lives in Ihosy, a town in south central Madagascar.

The observation of fady is also an important aspect of the traditional Malagasy belief system. Fady can relate to nearly anything in life—plants, animals, tombs, birds, or water, for example. Certain days are lucky for work or celebrations; others are disastrous for such purposes. Many fady stem from practical considerations of fertility and survival. Others come down through local legends and traditions. In addition, *mpisikidy* (local wise people) exercise their knowledge of plants and herbs for healing and for protection from harm or misfortune. *Mpanandro* (seers) advise people on their actions and have important roles in the daily life of the Malagasy.

The Arts and Recreation

Cultural life in Madagascar includes music, oral literature, theater, traditional sculpture, and crafts. The island's contact with many cultures has given it a rich diversity of artistic styles.

Among the Merina, for example, the *mpilalao*—musical troupes who wear lambas over their redingotes (fitted outer garments)—specialize in traditional songs and dances. These are often inspired by Bible stories and folk tales. The *valiha* is one of the most beautiful of all traditional Malagasy instruments and is the best accompaniment to Malagasy songs. The instrument has a long bamboo trunk with several fine metallic strings stretched across it that, when plucked, produce the sound.

Although wood carving is the primary art form on the island, a number of Malagasy painters, potters, and architects work in international styles. Local carvers produce small statues, inlaid plaques, and symbolic grave markers, called *aloala*.

Literary efforts have been concentrated in the areas of poetry and fiction writing. The greatest poet in Malagasy history is considered to be Jean-Joseph Rabearivelo, who died in 1937. Other well-known au-thors include Jacques Rabemananjara and Flavien Ranaivo. Economic difficulty and government censorship have curtailed the publication of the works of most modern Malagasy writers.

Several well-known sports—soccer (also called football), rugby, volleyball, and bas-ketball—are popular in Madagascar, and the country has produced some outstand-ing athletes. The national pastime, how-ever, is a game similar to checkers called *fanorona*, which is played on a board di-vided into 32 squares that are crossed by many diagonal lines.

A young girl carries on the traditions of her people by performing a local dance.

A Malagasy soldier and his driver play *fanorona*, a board game that is similar to checkers.

Courtesy of American Lutheran Church
Traditional village homes, such as these near Tolagnaro in southeastern Madagascar, are built with local materials.

Courtesy of American Lutheran Church
Using woven sieves, young Malagasy thresh a pile of rice in an east coast village.

Photo by Alton Halverson
A market in Antananarivo displays the area's variety of tropical fruits, which add diversity to the daily diet of the islanders.

Wearing a lamba, this Malagasy musician performs on a locally made stringed instrument.

Food, Clothing, and Housing

The Malagasy diet varies from region to region, according to what is produced locally. Rice is the most important food nearly everywhere on the island, except in some parts of the south and the west where maize (corn) and cassavas (fleshy root crops) are eaten. Sweet potatoes, co-

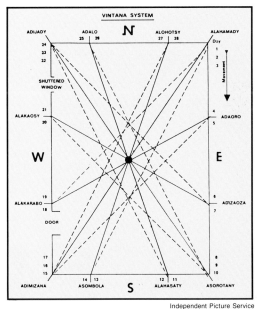

This diagram depicts the way in which traditional dwellings are built, using both religious beliefs and compass directions as guides.

conuts, tomatoes, beans, and tropical fruits and berries add some variety, along with a green vegetable called bredi that is similar to spinach. Coastal groups eat fish regularly.

Although beef, poultry, and pork are available, these meats are consumed only on special occasions. In addition, milk and eggs are rarely a part of the typical diet. Lack of these foods has led to widespread protein and vitamin deficiencies. The national drink is called *rano vola*, which is made by boiling water on top of the rice that sticks to the bottom of the cooking pot. Served hot or cold, rano vola is thirst-quenching.

A trip from one end of the country to the other would reveal the great variety of clothing worn by the Malagasy people. Men often wear a long gown called a *malabary*. The most common style, worn by both men and women, is the lamba, a long piece of cloth that is draped over the shoulders and across the chest. Along the west coast, women often wear sarongs (loose skirts).

Malagasy urban dwellings resemble those found in cities throughout the world. In villages, however, traditional houses are built according to Malagasy religious beliefs. Each direction has a special significance for the Malagasy people. Usually rectangular, a typical house runs from north to south, with the door facing the west. For some, the north represents power, the south suggests bad influences, and the east is sacred. As a result, the Malagasy sleep with their heads facing toward the east, never toward the south.

In the Central Highlands, most ordinary houses are made of brick or mud. Some are large and have two levels, while others are one-room homes. In the coastal areas, the walls and roofs of the dwellings are made of wood, bamboo, or fibers. Houses on the east coast may be built on stilts. Furnishings are simple, and a woven mat is used as a bed. Often there are no tables, chairs, or other furniture.

A worker walks through a neatly planted field of rice in a well-watered valley. Most of the rice cultivation occurs on small farms where the main labor is done by hand.

4) The Economy

After President Ratsiraka came to power in 1975, Madagascar's government began to operate certain industries and services that previously had been owned by private companies. Increased government control of the economy did not bring better times to the nation, however. The cost of oil and other imports soared. Because rice yields were so poor during the 1980s, Madagascar was forced to buy large amounts of that grain overseas. During the same period, sales of goods to foreign countries decreased.

In an attempt to correct this trade imbalance in the mid-1980s, the government changed some of its policies. It reduced state ownership and encouraged local and foreign investors to develop new industries that would produce goods for export. Madagascar sharply restricted imports in order to reduce the amount of money being spent abroad. This policy resulted in a scarcity of goods, and the cost of living in the cities tripled from 1987 to 1989.

Agriculture

Madagascar's economy is essentially agricultural, and nearly 80 percent of the people live in rural areas. Although 10 percent of the island's surface can be cultivated, only about 3 percent was under cultivation in the 1980s. Water is plentiful in most regions, but farming methods are most often old-fashioned. A long-handled spade is the principal tool.

Although the land usually is divided into small family plots, farmers share fields in some areas, and large plantations of sugarcane, cotton, cloves, and sisal (a fiber used in rope making) also exist. Most agricultural production for domestic consumption has not kept pace with the growth of the population, which has had trouble feeding itself in recent years.

The slash-and-burn method of clearing land—known as *tavy* in Madagascar— has been made illegal on the island because it destroys forests and erodes the soil. It is, however, still practiced by farmers throughout the island and endangers Malagasy animal and plant life. Irrigation on sloped terrain is difficult to manage, and many farmers produce barely enough to feed themselves and their families. Many rural Malagasy regard the additional acreages brought under cultivation through the tavy process as necessary for survival.

EXPORT CROPS

Coffee is the chief product of Madagascar's east coast and is also the most important export, accounting for more than half of the revenue brought in from foreign trade. In an average year, well over 50,000 tons of coffee are shipped to foreign ports. In spite of the importance of coffee to Madagascar's economy, only a few large plantations exist. The main source of coffee is the small-scale planter.

Second in importance as an export crop is vanilla, introduced into Madagascar in the middle of the nineteenth century. Vanilla cultivation has expanded so much along the east coast that Madagascar has long been the world's leading producer. Cloves, pepper, and lima beans are also important agricultural products in demand by foreign markets.

Independent Picture Service

The humid climate on Madagascar's east coast is ideal for growing clove trees. Here, laborers harvest the flower buds from which the spice is made.

Much emphasis is now being placed on cotton, which was brought to Madagascar in 1900 and which may be a valuable product if its cultivation is expanded. Most of the existing cotton fields are along the southwestern coast.

Independent Picture Service

Malagasy farmers still use long-handled spades to turn the soil for planting.

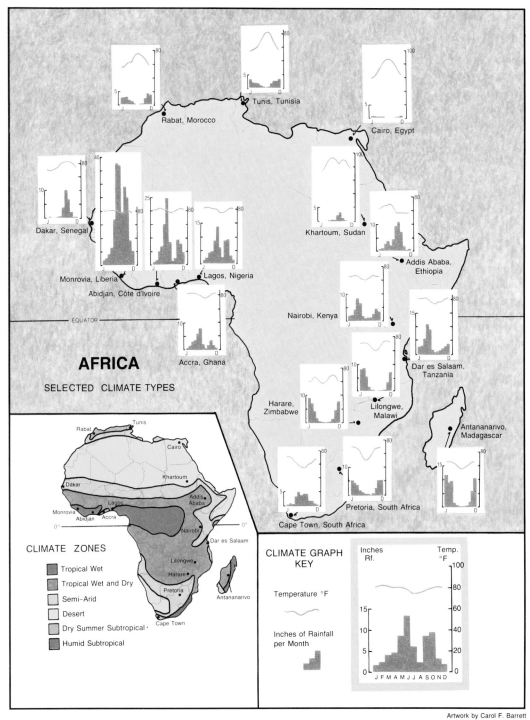

AFRICA

SELECTED CLIMATE TYPES

Rabat, Morocco

Tunis, Tunisia

Cairo, Egypt

Dakar, Senegal

Khartoum, Sudan

Monrovia, Liberia

Abidjan, Côte d'Ivoire

Lagos, Nigeria

Addis Ababa, Ethiopia

Nairobi, Kenya

Dar es Salaam, Tanzania

EQUATOR

Accra, Ghana

Harare, Zimbabwe

Lilongwe, Malawi

Antananarivo, Madagascar

Pretoria, South Africa

Cape Town, South Africa

CLIMATE ZONES

Tunis
Rabat
Cairo
Khartoum
Dakar
Addis Ababa
Lagos
Monrovia
Abidjan Accra
0°
Nairobi
0°
Dar es Salaam
Lilongwe
Harare
Pretoria
Antananarivo
Cape Town

- Tropical Wet
- Tropical Wet and Dry
- Semi–Arid
- Desert
- Dry Summer Subtropical
- Humid Subtropical

CLIMATE GRAPH KEY

Temperature °F

Inches of Rainfall per Month

Inches Rf.   Temp. °F

J F M A M J J A S O N D

Artwork by Carol F. Barrett

These climate graphs show the monthly change in the average rainfall and in the average temperature from January to December for the capital cities of 16 African nations. Antananarivo, Madagascar, has a tropical wet and dry climate, with a typically pronounced dry season during the winter (May through September). The capital's relatively mild temperatures, even in the summer months, are due to Antananarivo's location in the Ankaratra Massif, as well as to its nearness to the sea. Data taken from *World-Climates* by Willy Rudloff, Stuttgart, 1981.

Just outside the capital city of Antananarivo in the Central Highlands lie small rice paddies that produce part of the nation's basic food supply.

MAIN DOMESTIC CROPS

The most important crop is rice, which is grown mostly for home consumption, although a special high-quality variety has been developed for export. Since independence in 1960, the amount of land devoted to rice has doubled. Rice is grown in the Central Highlands by the Betsileo and the Merina, and in the east by the Betsimi-saraka and the Tanala. These groups cultivate rice in irrigated fields, in marshy areas that do not require irrigation, and on dry land or sloped terraces where the forest and bush have been burned off.

The entire rice-growing cycle—preparing the field, planting, replanting, cultivating, and harvesting—takes only from 120 to 150 days every year. During the 1980s,

Most of Madagascar's cassava crop, which is grown in large fields, is consumed locally.

however, many farmers chose not to grow rice, because the government set low prices for the grain to make it affordable to city dwellers. Shortages of this food staple grew worse when cyclones destroyed most of the crop in 1982, 1984, 1986, and 1987. As a result, Madagascar has had to rely on costly imports of rice.

The second largest crop is cassava, which fills in as the staple food in the Malagasy diet during years of poor rice harvests. Most of the cassava crop is consumed locally, but some is processed and exported as starch and as tapioca.

Introduced into Madagascar in about 1800, sugarcane can be grown in any area that has an altitude of less than 4,000 feet. Most of the sugar plantations, however, are along the northwestern coast, especially on the island of Noissi-Bé. Much of the crop is sold abroad, making sugar the fourth most important export item. Small-scale farmers also grow their own sugarcane on little plots and frequently use it to make a fermented drink called *betsabetsa*.

Zebu cows, with their characteristic hump, quench their thirst at a waterway in southern Madagascar.

Women beat stalks of grain against a tree stump to separate the edible kernels from the stems and seed coverings.

LIVESTOCK

Several hundred years ago, African hump-backed cattle were imported to the island. Called zebu, they now number over 10 million and make up most of the cattle population. Some zebu are used as labor animals for plowing and hauling. Even though zebu cattle are symbols of wealth and status, some are sacrificed for family ceremonies, religious festivals, and other purposes. These offerings, although they diminish the herd, also bring prestige.

Pigs, first brought to the island by early Portuguese explorers, are frequently seen. Sheep are raised mostly in the extreme southwest. In the south and west, Angora goats provide milk as well as the raw material for mohair yarn. Geese, ducks, and chickens are kept by most villagers, supplying eggs and meat for family celebrations.

Photo by Alton Halverson

Mica, a thin metal that appears in its natural state as nearly transparent, leaflike fragments, is used, after refinement, as electrical insulation and as fireproofing material.

Fishing and Mining

Although few Malagasy take to the sea to exploit the rich resources off the island's coastline, the Vezo and other small populations have lived from the profits of fishing for generations. The inland diet is sometimes enriched by fish, which is cooked with the daily rice. Recently, trawling for shellfish has become an important industry. As a result, shrimp is now one of Madagascar's leading export commodities.

Madagascar has been called a "land of samples" because so many different kinds of minerals exist on the island, but only in limited quantities. Small gold deposits have been found in the north near Antsiranana, but only modest amounts have been recovered. Some people in the area practice gold panning. Although estimates indicate that low-grade coal reserves of over 700 million tons exist in the Sakao River area, mining has not yet begun.

Madagascar is one of the world's largest producers of graphite. First discovered in the highlands, new veins have now been found south of Antananarivo. This mineral is used chiefly in the electronics industry,

Courtesy of American Lutheran Church

Although fishing has yet to become a major industry, this Malagasy youth adds his catch to the family's selection of foods.

but the demand for it has lessened in recent years.

Chromium (from which chrome is made) is another very important mineral, and as much as 105,000 tons have been exported in a year, particularly to the United States. World demand for the mineral has declined in the 1980s, however, and recent production has been only 40,000 to 50,000 tons. Deposits of mica (a thin, transparent metal) are found chiefly in the south, but demand for it is low. Other mineral resources include bauxite (from which aluminum is made), phosphate, uranium, and thorium (a radioactive element), plus valuable nickel deposits near Moramanga.

Madagascar is probably best known, however, for its semiprecious stones, found in great variety and quantity. The most popular stones are amethysts, beryls, garnets, moonstones, and tourmalines.

Industry

Most Malagasy industries—such as sugar refining, textile production, tobacco curing, meat preserving, and leather tanning—are closely tied to agricultural products. Cotton weaving takes place in privately owned plants, but most of Madagascar's industry is in government hands. Sugar is milled on the northwestern coast, on the island of Noissi-Bé, and in the port city of Mahajanga.

Factories process peanuts for food and for cooking oil. In the south, where sisal is grown, textile and rope-making works have been opened. Silk weaving and furniture making are minor industries. Craftspeople produce pottery, lace, baskets, and rugs, and the government has established a special crafts agency to encourage these endeavors. Other light industries produce goods such as matches, shoes, hats, plastics, soap, cement, elastics, and soft drinks —all for the local market. Yet Madagascar's industrial output continues to be very limited, and the economy suffers regularly from shortages of basic supplies. As a result, a very active black market (illegal trade in goods) thrives throughout the island.

A Malagasy artisan weaves a piece of fabric out of mohair (goats' wool) in Ampanihy, southern Madagascar.

Recently harvested sisal stalks arrive at a factory in Berenty, southern Madagascar.

Five-foot-long sisal fibers are draped over a frame to make them easy to move.

After enough fibers have been collected, they are left in the sun to dry. Dried sisal can be woven into rope or matting.

An experienced brickmaker packs locally available clay into molds, which are left in the sun to dry.

Few pieces of modern machinery are produced in Madagascar, and even imported apparatuses sometimes are idle for lack of spare parts.

Energy and Transportation

Potential sites for the production of water-power are plentiful on Madagascar, and two large dams supply electricity near Antananarivo. Other known sources of energy —coal, lignite (a rougher form of coal), and oil sands (sandstone from which petroleum is extracted)—remained untapped until the early 1980s. Instead, harvests from precious forests provided fuel. Even in places where other types of fuels are available, firewood continues to be the principal energy source for domestic use.

Crude oil is imported from the Middle East and is refined at Toamasina, although the refinery's sales have declined in recent years. The country's hydroelectrical facilities, concentrated near urban centers like Antananarivo, supply only 20 percent of national energy needs. Thermal plants also provide a small amount of power.

A road network now covers a total distance of 22,000 miles, but as yet only 2,500 miles are tarred. Most of the roads are not surfaced at all, and paved roads are in poor condition. As a result, many small towns are isolated during the rainy season.

Madagascar has 532 miles of narrow-gauge railway. The main section, opened in 1909, runs from Antananarivo to Toa-masina, and branches travel north to the Lake Alaotra region and south to Antsirabe. A section also runs from Fianarantsoa to Manakara on the east coast.

Air transportation is extremely important, and Air Madagascar serves many communities. Five airports on the island are large enough to take jet aircraft, and flights travel directly from Antananarivo to Europe, Africa, and the nearby islands of Réunion, Mauritius, and the Comoros.

For hundreds of years, the Malagasy transported everything by foot, carrying goods at both ends of a pole that rested on their shoulders. Today most people travel by *taxi-be*, a large car holding 7 or 8 passengers, or by *taxi-brousse*, a local bus seating about 20 with standing room for as many as can be crowded in. Some of these buses travel long distances and will carry anything—people, hens, goats, or baskets of fish.

Trading and Tourism

During the 1980s, Madagascar had an unfavorable trading situation. Shortages of food and other necessities forced the country to spend more money on imports from abroad. At the same time, however, world

During the rainy season, many of the island's smaller roads are washed out and are passable only on foot.

demand for Madagascar's products—including coffee, cloves, and vanilla—declined. In an attempt to balance foreign spending and earnings, the government began a program that severely restricted imports.

The nation was also deeply in debt and had to make payments on money it had borrowed from the International Monetary Fund (IMF)—a lending agency linked to the United Nations. In 1983 the IMF agreed to extend Madagascar's loan payments if the country changed the way it operated its economy. The IMF required Madagascar to reduce spending on social programs—such as health and education—and to sell most of the companies it had acquired since Ratsiraka came to power in 1975. In 1988 the nation sold 300 state-controlled firms back to private owners. By 1989 it was still uncertain whether privately owned businesses would be able to increase the sale of Madagascar's products on world markets.

Wood, cut from Madagascar's dwindling forests, is the main source of household fuel.

At present, most imports and exports are exchanged between Madagascar and France or other members of the European Economic Community. Trade with Great Britain is minimal, but the United States buys about 24 percent of Madagascar's exports. All products for export must be shipped a long distance, which is a handicap because of the high cost of freight.

After flight routes developed between Madagascar and Europe and Africa, the government made a special effort to attract tourists. The idea was revived in the late 1980s, after more than a decade in which few visitors came to the island. Although somewhat shabby, with few modern conveniences and many shortages of goods, Madagascar has many attractive assets. The capital, Antananarivo, has a number of hotels and restaurants as well as various extraordinary sights and customs. Rare wildlife and plants are also of interest to visitors. Perhaps the island's most attractive feature is its nearly perfect climate throughout the year.

The Future

Despite its economic promise, unusual environment, and cultural strengths, Madagascar struggles for survival. Poverty, underdevelopment, and rigid state control hamper the island's progress. Madagascar is dependent on the industrialized markets

Courtesy of American Lutheran Church

Madagascar's sunny climate and excellent beaches draw more visitors each year. As a result, tourism has become an important source of the island's income.

Two young Malagasy display the friendship and affection that has often been lacking among the island's peoples. Future generations may yet find a way to unify Madagascar's fragmented society to achieve greater progress and prosperity.

of Western Europe and the United States, and it has not been able to expand its own industries. Although it has a farm-based economy and abundant land, Madagascar is continually short of food. Unchecked timber cutting threatens vast forests, and wildlife species have been disappearing at a rapid rate.

In addition, the island is fragmented into many regions and factions. National roads and other economic links are as poor as they were at independence in 1960. And the Malagasy remain divided among themselves—into urban and rural inhabitants, into educated elites and underprivileged poor, into government supporters and uncompromising opponents. No government has ever unified all of these subgroups in an effective way. Madagascar is in deep debt to foreign banks and organizations, and it must follow economic rules designed by its creditors.

The outlook is somewhat discouraging for a republic that is not fully able to follow its own course in foreign or economic affairs. But the Malagasy still control their own future and hope to preserve the uniqueness of their culture.

63

Index